**CORNERSTONES OF FREEDOM**™

# WOMEN'S RIGHT TO VOTE

BY PETER BENOIT

**CHILDREN'S PRESS**®
An Imprint of Scholastic Inc.
New York  Toronto  London  Auckland  Sydney
Mexico City  New Delhi  Hong Kong
Danbury, Connecticut

BRINGING
HISTORY
to LIFE

Content Consultant
James Marten, PhD
Professor and Chair, History Department
Marquette University
Milwaukee, Wisconsin

Library of Congress Cataloging-in-Publication Data
Benoit, Peter.
 Women's right to vote / by Peter Benoit.
  pages cm
 Includes bibliographical references and index.
 ISBN 978-0-531-21333-9 (lib. bdg.) — ISBN 978-0-531-25829-3 (pbk.)
 1. Women—Suffrage—United States—History—Juvenile literature. I.
Title.
 JK1898.W65 2014
 324.6′230973—dc23                    2013030655

SCHOLASTIC, CHILDREN'S PRESS, CORNERSTONES OF FREEDOM™,
and associated logos are trademarks and/or registered trademarks of
Scholastic Inc.

1 2 3 4 5 6 7 8 9 10 R 23 22 21 20 19 18 17 16 15 14

Photographs ©: AP Images/North Wind Picture Archives: 8, 19; Corbis
Images: 4 bottom, 5 bottom, 20, 24, 37, 41 (Bettmann), 46; Getty Images:
49 (American Stock), cover (APA), 27 (Fotosearch), 7 (Justin Sullivan),
30 (Kean Collection), 16 (Kean Collection/Hulton Archive), 44 (Paul
Thompson/Topical Press Agency), 28 (Stock Montage), 14, 56 top (Time
& Life Pictures), 50 (Topical Press Agency); Library of Congress: back
cover, 48; Newscom: 6 (Erik S. Lesser/EPA), 32 (Everett Collection), 18
(Jenny Stock Connection Worldwide); North Wind Picture Archives: 35;
Science Source: 25; Shutterstock, Inc./Harry Hu: 55; Superstock, Inc.: 31
(DeAgostini), 2, 3, 23, 34, 38, 40, 42, 47, 56 bottom, 57 (Everett Collection),
29 (Huntington Library/DeAgostini); The Granger Collection: 11, 15, 36;
The Image Works: 22, 54 (akg-images), 4 top, 10, 26 (North Wind Picture
Archives), 17 (Syracuse Newspapers/L. Long); Thinkstock: 5 top, 13.

Maps by XNR Productions, Inc.

# Did you know that studying history can be fun?

**BRING HISTORY TO LIFE** by becoming a history investigator. Examine the evidence (primary and secondary source materials); cross-examine the people and witnesses. Take a look at what was happening at the time—but be careful! What happened years ago might suddenly become incredibly interesting and change the way you think!

# Contents

# SETTING THE SCENE

# Deciding an Election

**Today, politicians must secure support from female voters in order to win elections.**

Women play an important role in modern politics. In the 2012 U.S. presidential election, they accounted for 53 percent of all voters. President Barack Obama won

**MORE WOMEN THAN MEN VOTED IN EACH**

the election in part by securing more than half of the votes cast by women. If his competitor, Mitt Romney, had won that many votes from women, he would likely have won the election.

In light of this outcome, it is easy to forget that women have not always held such power. Until 1920, there was no national law guaranteeing women the right to vote. As a result, many states barred women from participating in elections. Women fought hard to win the right to help choose their leaders. Their eventual success came only after decades of struggle and sacrifice.

**Mitt Romney took several political positions that were unpopular among female voters, leading in part to his defeat in the 2012 presidential election.**

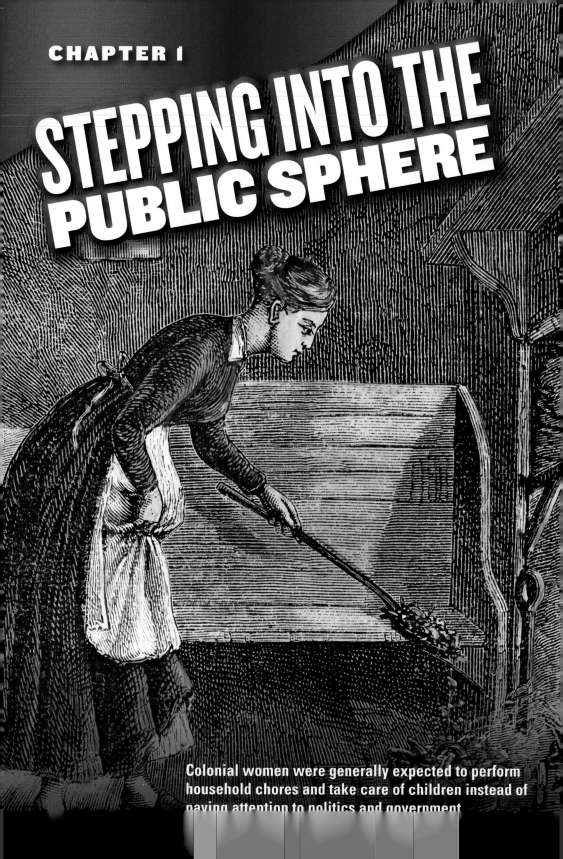

## CHAPTER 1

# STEPPING INTO THE PUBLIC SPHERE

Colonial women were generally expected to perform household chores and take care of children instead of paying attention to politics and government.

IN ORDER TO WIN THE RIGHT to vote, American **suffragists** had to fight against oppression that had been in place since the nation's earliest days. Before the United States was officially founded in 1776, it was a group of British colonies. In the colonies, women did not often have a say in local government. In many cases, they could not even own property. They were expected to obey their husbands and keep quiet about political issues.

Abigail Adams was well known for writing letters and having long discussions with friends about political issues of the time.

## An Unequal Society

Even though women were barred from participating in government, they still paid attention to the politics of the time. In 1776, colonial leaders were preparing to issue the Declaration of Independence. This document would proclaim the colonies to be a new nation, separate from Great Britain. John Adams, who would later serve as the second president of the United States, was one of the men working to create the declaration. His wife, Abigail Adams, wrote him a letter asking him to "remember the ladies" as he worked to draft the document that would outline the founding principles of the United States.

John Adams dismissed his wife's request. Writing to Massachusetts lawmaker James Sullivan around the same time, Adams detailed his concerns about women's suffrage. Adams believed that women were incapable of making up their own minds on whom to vote for. He argued that women would simply vote for the candidates their husbands, fathers, or brothers told them to.

John Adams's argument reflected the limited role of women in colonial society. Unmarried women were under the control of their fathers. Married women had to answer to their husbands. The law treated a couple as if they were one person, and that person was the

Once married, colonial women lost most of their individual rights and were largely placed under the control of their husbands.

# YESTERDAY'S HEADLINES

In 1756, Josiah Taft of Uxbridge, Massachusetts, passed away. With the French and Indian War imminent, the town of Uxbridge voted on taxes to be levied for the war effort. Taft had always paid the largest tax in Uxbridge. In an effort to provide him representation, town officials gave his widow, Lydia, the vote at the town meeting. As far as historians know, Lydia Taft was the only woman allowed to vote during the colonial era. The special circumstances that led to her being given a vote reveal the way men viewed women. Women would face many such struggles as they attempted to secure the right to vote.

husband. Married women could not enter into contracts of any type and could not own land. If a woman worked outside the home, she was required to give her wages to her husband. The practice of granting a husband control over his wife's legal rights was known as **coverture**.

## Under the Constitution

The U.S. Constitution, fully adopted by 1790, outlined the responsibilities and workings of the new nation's government. It defined both men and women as citizens. However, it did not spell out voting requirements. It stated only that elected representatives would be chosen by "the People of the several States." The details of voting were left to individual states. Many people were excluded from participating in government, including enslaved people and men who did not own property. The exact laws varied from state to state.

Because of coverture, most leaders believed that giving married women the right to vote would be like giving each man an extra vote. As a result, almost all states denied women the right to vote. New Jersey was the sole exception. Under its state constitution, women who owned enough property and met residence

**The U.S. Constitution granted control over voting and many other important subjects to the individual states rather than the federal government. As a result, voting laws could be very different from one state to another.**

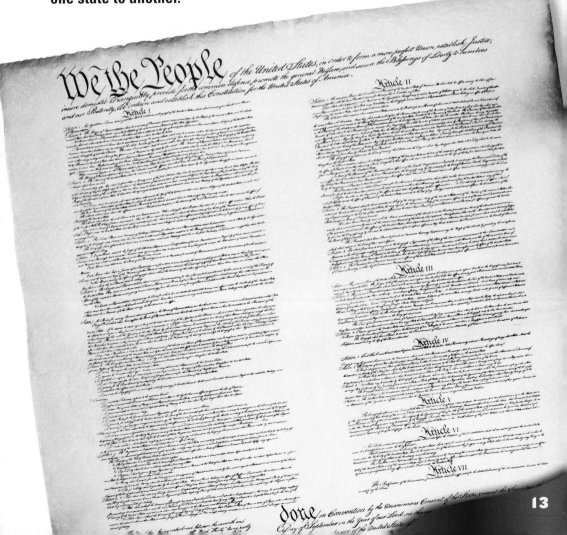

requirements could vote. However, married women owned no property due to coverture. Unmarried women were unlikely to acquire enough property to qualify for the vote. As a result, only wealthy widows voted in New Jersey. No other state allowed even this. However, this small victory did not last long. In 1807, several young men in one New Jersey county were accused of dressing as women and voting twice. This scandal caused the state **legislature** to take away women's voting rights.

## The First Steps

Little changed until the 1830s. Around this time, small groups of women began working to give married women more control over their property. At the time, American jobs were changing. Previously, most men had worked near their homes as farmers or craftsmen.

**Lucretia Mott first took an interest in women's rights after beginning a job as a teacher, for which she was paid just half the amount that male teachers at her school were paid.**

**Elizabeth Cady Stanton became interested in women's rights after learning about legal inequalities between men and women from her father, a U.S. congressman.**

By the 1830s, many of them were traveling to jobs away from the home. They were sometimes away for many months at a time. Wives needed the authority to run the household in their absence. However, the outdated laws of coverture made this difficult. Slowly, state by state, women convinced legislators of the need to expand their rights. The first Married Women's Property Act was passed by the Mississippi legislature in 1839. It gave women the right to control property and make contracts. Other states soon followed in Mississippi's path.

Women's newfound activism soon spread beyond property rights. Many began taking an interest in such issues as **temperance** and the **abolition** of slavery. In 1840, two women, Lucretia Mott and Elizabeth Cady Stanton, attended an international antislavery conference with their husbands. However, the conference's organizers declared the women

"constitutionally unfit" to participate. When noted abolitionist William Lloyd Garrison arrived, he was offended that the women had been excluded. In protest, he spent the conference talking with Mott and Stanton. They began to discuss the idea of a convention where women could organize a **reform** movement.

## Seneca Falls

The planned conference did not take shape until 1848, when Mott began to discuss it with her sister, Martha Coffin Wright. Along with Stanton and Mary M'Clintock, Mott and Wright met at the home of Jane Hunt in Waterloo, New York. Together, they planned an event "for protest and discussion." The women finalized the convention for July 19 and 20 at the Wesleyan Chapel in Seneca Falls, New York. They also drafted a document called the Declaration of Sentiments.

Modeled on the Declaration of Independence, it detailed the women's specific complaints about the male-dominated U.S. government.

When the 300 attendees arrived at the chapel on July 19, they found it locked. Some of the attendees lifted Stanton's nephew Daniel through a window, and he unlocked the chapel door. Inside, the Declaration of Sentiments was read slowly, discussed at length, and altered slightly. On the second day, 100 people signed the document, including 32 men. However, giving women the right to vote was by far the most controversial proposal in the declaration. Several men stormed out in protest when the attendees approved that part of the declaration.

Today, the site of the Seneca Falls Convention is part of the Women's Rights National Historical Park.

NEW YORK
FIRST CONVENTION FOR
WOMAN'S RIGHTS
WAS HELD ON THIS CORNER
1848
STATE EDUCATION
DEPARTMENT 1932

# A FIRSTHAND LOOK AT
## THE DECLARATION OF SENTIMENTS

The Declaration of Sentiments is one of our nation's most important documents. It detailed many of the ways women were treated unfairly by the U.S. government and acted as a framework for change. See page 60 for a link to read the declaration online.

The reaction in newspapers was mixed. Some editorials suggested that a women's rights movement would cause traditional family life to unravel. On the other side, Horace Greeley of the *New York Tribune*

**The Declaration of Sentiments and the names of its signers are engraved on a wall at the Women's Rights National Historical Park.**

SIGNERS OF THE DECLARATION OF SENTIMENTS

Seneca Falls, New York 19—

claimed that denying women "equal participation with men in political rights" was unreasonable. The following Sunday, ministers verbally attacked the Seneca Falls Convention in sermons. Signers of the Declaration of Sentiments were mocked without mercy. Some requested their signatures be removed from the declaration because of the harassment. However, most signers stood strong against the ministers. They began planning for future conventions. A bridge had been crossed, and there would be no turning back.

# TODAY'S PERSPECTIVE

The Seneca Falls Convention immediately generated major controversy. Many abolitionists embraced the movement because it promised to change voting laws. They saw this as a potential way for former slaves to gain voting rights as well. Ministers railed against the convention, and newspapers were divided in their opinions. Some people believed that empowering women would cause divorces or overturn existing laws of coverture. Others welcomed women's suffrage as a social advancement. For decades afterward, suffragists were criticized by their opponents. Today, women's suffrage and political equality with men is largely seen as the only fair and acceptable way of ruling the nation.

## CHAPTER 2
# A GRANDER STAGE

After gaining her own freedom, Sojourner Truth successfully sued for the freedom of her young son.

AS REMARKABLE AS THE Seneca Falls Convention had been, it was only a beginning. In May 1850, the Anti-Slavery Society held a meeting in Boston. Several suffragists attending that meeting planned a Women's Rights Convention for October 23 and 24 in Worcester, Massachusetts. Nearly 1,000 people attended the convention. Speakers addressed a number of suffragists' concerns, including equal access to jobs for women. An attendee named Lucy Stone urged changes in property laws. Sojourner Truth, a former slave who had escaped to freedom in 1826, spoke about the struggles faced by slave women. Worcester native Abby Kelley took the ultimate step, arguing that all social distinctions between men and women should be abolished.

In the early years of her work to secure equal rights for women, Susan B. Anthony was criticized heavily by many U.S. newspapers.

## A Growing Movement

The Women's Rights Convention drew a great deal of attention from newspapers. Most of it was negative. The *New York Herald* claimed that suffragists wanted to abolish both the Bible and the Constitution. It also stated that suffragists hoped to elect Abby Kelley as president of the United States. Other papers were all too willing to follow the *Herald*'s lead. This negative press only drew more attention to the suffragists, however. The movement was growing. Women's rights groups began forming in each of the states. Many held their own conventions.

Throughout the 1850s, women's suffrage often drew support and inspiration from abolitionists. Sojourner Truth delivered a powerful speech, titled "Ain't I a Woman?", at the 1851 Ohio Women's Convention. The speech revealed how closely issues of race and gender were tied together. However, as the suffrage movement grew in numbers and spread from the Northeast to other parts of the country, it took on a distinct identity.

The success of the movement depended on the tireless leadership of Lucy Stone, Susan B. Anthony, and Elizabeth Cady Stanton. Women learned through trial and error how to organize conventions, raise funds, and manage finances. They led **petition** drives and pressed for legislative hearings. They also collected money at lectures and meetings and used it to print books. These publications helped spread far and wide the goals of suffragists.

Susan B. Anthony (left) and Elizabeth Cady Stanton (right) worked together closely to provide leadership for the growing women's rights movement.

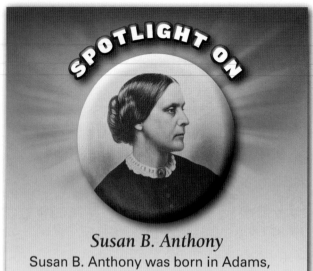

### Susan B. Anthony

Susan B. Anthony was born in Adams, Massachusetts, in 1820. In the late 1830s, her family moved to Rochester, New York. There, she became immersed in the fight to abolish slavery. In 1851, Anthony met Elizabeth Cady Stanton at an antislavery conference. Soon, the two combined their talents in support of women's rights. For more than 50 years, Anthony fought for women's right to vote. In 1905, she even met with President Theodore Roosevelt to speak in support of an amendment for women's suffrage. However, she died a year later, her dream not yet realized.

## Women During War

When the Civil War erupted in April 1861, the women's suffrage movement faded from public view. At the same time, women continued to take on new roles in society. Women in both the North and South volunteered their talents and energies to the war effort. Everywhere, women sewed and laundered uniforms. They planted and canned fruits and vegetables, and they raised money for medical supplies.

Some volunteered as nurses in hospitals near the front lines of the war. In all, 20,000 women directly aided the Union army alone. In June 1861, the U.S. government established an organization to prevent the spread of disease in army camps and hospitals. Women raised several million dollars for supplies.

**More than 600,000 soldiers were killed fighting in the Civil War.**

Stanton and Anthony were encouraged by women's expanding roles during the war. In 1863, they called for a meeting of "Loyal Women" to "lay hold of their birthright of freedom." At the meeting, leaders discussed both the abolition of slavery and women's suffrage. They also discussed their support of voting rights for freed slaves. The attendees formed a group called the Women's Loyal National League to help push these issues forward. The league ultimately collected more than 400,000 signatures on a petition to end slavery. After the war ended in 1865, it also helped encourage Congress to pass the 13th Amendment, which made slavery illegal in the United States.

**While the 14th and 15th Amendments took important steps forward by granting citizenship and voting rights to formerly enslaved men, they continued to restrict women from equal participation in government.**

However, the league met with resistance when it began to push for women's suffrage as well. Abolitionists worried that pushing too hard for women's suffrage would weaken the chances of winning suffrage for freed slaves. A rift between the two causes seemed unavoidable. In spite of this, supporters of women's suffrage and black suffrage came together to establish the American Equal Rights Association (AERA) in May 1866.

A few weeks later, Congress passed the 14th Amendment, which limited citizenship rights specifically to men. Suffragists felt defeated. In February 1869, Congress passed the 15th Amendment. It guaranteed that voting rights could not be denied based on "race, color, or previous condition of servitude." However, it still allowed for voting rights to be denied based on gender. AERA leader Lucy Stone supported the amendment's **ratification**. Anthony and Stanton, however, were unhappy with the amendment. They believed it had harmed the chances for women's suffrage. As a result, AERA split into two separate groups. Anthony and Stanton formed a new group called the National Woman Suffrage Association (NWSA). Stone and other supporters of the 15th Amendment formed the American Woman Suffrage Association (AWSA).

**When she married in 1855, Lucy Stone refused to take her husband's last name in protest of the unfair treatment of married women.**

As women gained the right to vote in states such as Wyoming, they began turning up at the polls in large numbers to cast their ballots.

## One State at a Time

The AWSA committed itself to securing suffrage by campaigning for state-by-state reform of voting laws. It sponsored lectures, distributed suffrage literature, and established state and local societies. By the year's end, Wyoming **Territory** had granted women's suffrage.

Utah Territory followed in 1870. However, pushing women's suffrage through state legislatures was costly, and the AWSA's work stalled. It would be 23 years before Colorado granted suffrage.

On election day in 1872, Susan B. Anthony headed to the polls in Rochester, New York, and cast her votes. She was arrested soon afterward. Anthony argued that the 14th Amendment had already granted women the right to vote. The amendment stated that "All persons born or naturalized in the United States" were citizens. Because

In Susan B. Anthony's 1873 trial for voting illegally, the judge wrote out his guilty verdict before Anthony even had the chance to present her case.

# SUSAN B. ANTHONY'S 1874 PETITION TO CONGRESS

In 1874, Susan B. Anthony petitioned Congress to remove the fine she had been punished with two years earlier for voting illegally. In her petition, she argued that the punishment was unjust. See page 60 for a link to read the petition online.

the Constitution gave citizens the right to vote, Anthony argued, it was unconstitutional to deny women their rights. When Anthony presented her argument in court, the all-male jury disagreed with her. She was fined $100 for voting illegally. Anthony refused to pay.

Other women embraced Anthony's method, with similar results. Virginia Minor was turned away when she attempted

**Virginia Minor played a major role in relief efforts during the Civil War.**

to register to vote in Missouri in 1872. Her husband, an attorney, challenged the restriction in *Minor v. Happersett.* He argued that voting was her 14th Amendment right as a U.S. citizen. The Missouri state courts disagreed. The U.S. Supreme Court reviewed the state ruling in 1875. In a crushing blow for women's suffrage, the court held that voting rights were not guaranteed to all citizens by the Constitution. This ruling narrowed the options available to suffragists. They could either work to have state laws reformed one at a time or amend the Constitution.

# YESTERDAY'S HEADLINES

Susan B. Anthony, Elizabeth Cady Stanton, and Matilda Gage wrote a Declaration of Rights that they hoped to present at the 1876 Philadelphia Centennial Exposition (above) on July 4, following a public reading of the Declaration of Independence.

After the Declaration of Independence had been read, Anthony and four other women showed their Declaration of Rights to the man in charge of the show. Though he refused to let them present it, Anthony went to a platform and spoke to a large crowd. She said that because women were not allowed to vote, they were denied the rights that the Founding Fathers had argued for in the Declaration of Independence. Anthony's speech captured the attention of the press as well as thousands of people in attendance.

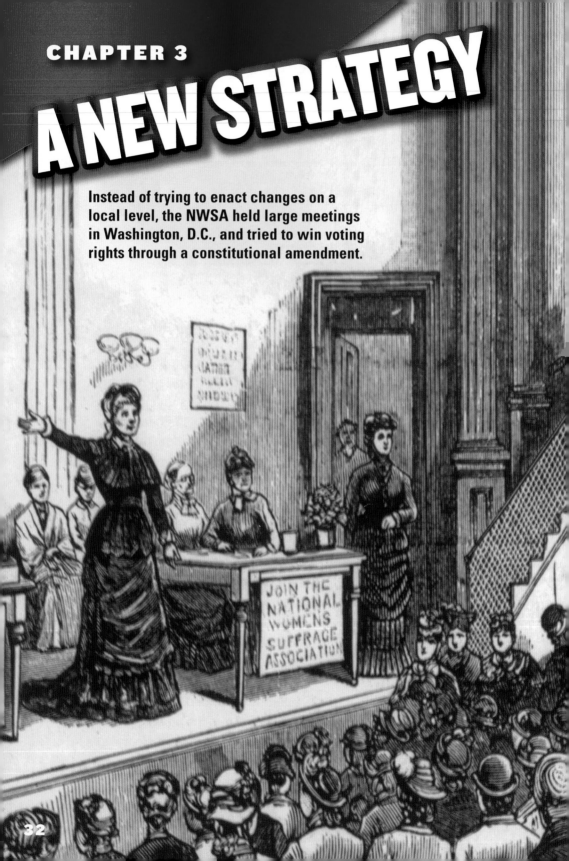

## CHAPTER 3

# A NEW STRATEGY

Instead of trying to enact changes on a local level, the NWSA held large meetings in Washington, D.C., and tried to win voting rights through a constitutional amendment.

JOIN THE
NATIONAL
WOMENS
SUFFRAGE
ASSOCIATION

IN 1878, NWSA SUFFRAGISTS proposed a constitutional amendment granting women the right to vote. Unsurprisingly, it failed to get congressional approval. The same proposed amendment was introduced and turned down in every congressional session for the following 41 years. Virginia Minor's case had made it clear that the Supreme Court was unwilling to place voting among the Constitution's "privileges and immunities." As a result, the AWSA adopted the strategy of winning voting rights state by state.

## Public Perception

Suffragists struggled against the negative reputation they had among much of the public. Women supporting the cause were considered outrageous. Their behavior seemed dangerously at odds with traditional views of women's roles. Suffragists were not submissive to men. They were not satisfied to spend all of their time doing household chores and taking care of children. As a result, their opponents suggested that they were not true women.

Despite these obstacles, the women's suffrage movement began to grow again in the early 1880s. This growth was thanks in part to Frances Willard. Willard was the president of the Woman's Christian Temperance Union (WCTU). She had an enormous obstacle to overcome. Since the middle of the 19th century, popular magazines had helped to spread a specific understanding of womanhood. These

**Frances Willard became known for her skills at achieving goals through political dealings.**

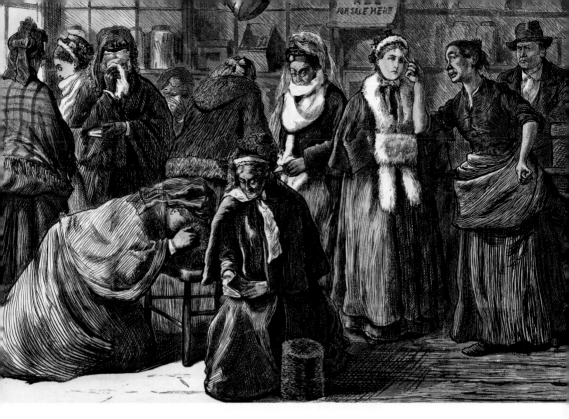

**Supporters of temperance sometimes took over saloons to protest alcohol consumption.**

publications claimed that a true woman was religious and submissive. Her proper place was in the home, not in the workplace or the political world. Married women were discouraged from working outside the home, and few did. By 1880, Willard and the WCTU had begun to question this narrow view of womanhood.

The descriptions of the "true woman" that women read about in magazines had little in common with their day-to-day struggles. As the number of saloons increased, husbands took to drinking, with disastrous consequences. Many of them drank too much and became violent. Sometimes the women were even left to raise children on their own when their husbands left

**Hull House, founded by suffragist Jane Addams, offered music classes and other activities for local children.**

them. Without jobs, these women were unable to meet the expense of raising a family.

## The New Woman

Some women fought for temperance by protesting against the saloons where men often drank. Others, including Frances Willard, decided that the best way to solve the issues women faced was to support women's suffrage. Willard believed that if women could vote, they could help pass new laws to prevent husbands from drinking too much and treating their families poorly. Her campaign for suffrage was called the Home Protection Ballot. It helped spread the idea that a true woman should also be a voter.

Freed from the restrictive roles men had made for them, women dedicated themselves to changing the world directly. Some, like suffragist Jane Addams, worked to establish **settlement houses** in the cities. Addams's Hull House was established in Chicago in 1889. It was a place where newly arrived foreigners could begin their transition into American life. Hull House provided health care and fought to reform child labor laws and improve the education system. The women of Hull House were also active in the suffrage movement. Addams became the "new woman," who combined the traditional woman's role with political reform.

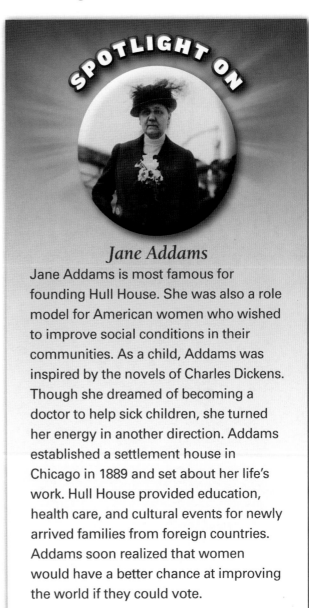

SPOTLIGHT ON

*Jane Addams*

Jane Addams is most famous for founding Hull House. She was also a role model for American women who wished to improve social conditions in their communities. As a child, Addams was inspired by the novels of Charles Dickens. Though she dreamed of becoming a doctor to help sick children, she turned her energy in another direction. Addams established a settlement house in Chicago in 1889 and set about her life's work. Hull House provided education, health care, and cultural events for newly arrived families from foreign countries. Addams soon realized that women would have a better chance at improving the world if they could vote.

## High Society

Though many WCTU members had dedicated themselves to women's suffrage, many more had not. In 1890, the NWSA and AWSA merged to form the National American Woman Suffrage Association (NAWSA). Its creation led to a rebirth of the suffrage movement. NAWSA suffragists knew that most American women remained indifferent to their cause. Their opponents recruited members from high society, complicating the suffragists' efforts to gain respect for their position. Under the leadership of Carrie Chapman Catt, NAWSA reached out to society women to increase the movement's respectability. This strategy met some resistance from women who thought that it excluded lower social classes

**Before Carrie Chapman Catt was married in 1890, her husband signed a legally binding contract guaranteeing that she would have at least four months of free time each year to devote to the fight for voting rights.**

from the movement. However, NAWSA's plan helped lead to a new and improved image for suffragists.

At the turn of the century, NAWSA leaders began sponsoring events called College Evenings. These events were meant to broaden the movement's appeal for young, educated women. NAWSA helped to develop histories of women's suffrage and libraries where books about the movement's pioneers could inspire young women. The new approach was a stunning success. NAWSA membership stood at 12,000 in 1906. Four years later, it was at 117,000.

This success brought results in the struggle for women's suffrage. Between 1893 and 1911, five additional states— Colorado (1893), Utah (1896), Idaho (1896), Washington (1910), and California (1911)—gave women the vote.

## Women in the Workplace

In 1908, the Supreme Court upheld an Oregon court's ruling in *Muller v. Oregon*. The ruling reformed labor laws to make the workplace safer for women. The decision was a victory for women's labor law reform, but a roadblock for suffrage. The court ruled that women should not be allowed to work long hours. It argued that women were less able to meet the workplace's physical demands than men were. Suffragists saw a danger in this ruling. If the court could discriminate based on gender in labor laws, then it might do the same thing with voting laws. Suffragists feared that the Supreme Court would overturn the state laws that had given some women the vote.

**Many women began working at factory jobs in the early 20th century.**

The *Muller* ruling convinced suffragists more than ever that a constitutional amendment would be needed to secure voting rights for all women. In 1907, the movement

## A FIRSTHAND LOOK AT
### MULLER V. OREGON

*Muller v. Oregon* was a landmark labor law ruling. However, the victory came with a steep price for suffragists. By discriminating between sexes, the Supreme Court set an example that it could potentially overturn state laws guaranteeing women suffrage. See page 60 for a link to read the court's ruling online.

was energized when a group of British suffragists visited New York. These suffragists met with Harriot Stanton Blatch, the daughter of Elizabeth Cady Stanton. Blatch firmly believed that the suffrage movement's success depended on support from working women. She created a group called the Equality League to involve these women in the fight for suffrage.

The Equality League was founded on the idea that NAWSA's efforts did not give the movement the broad visibility it needed to succeed. British suffragists were more **militant** than their American counterparts. Because of their influence, the American suffragists organized parades, **picketed**, and spoke in public places to mobilize large crowds. The press could not ignore the growing movement. Women had spoken, and at last their voices were heard!

# YESTERDAY'S HEADLINES

British suffragists brought new tactics to their American allies. Suffrage demonstrations led to expanded press coverage, and the suffragists' stories raised interest and created sympathy for the demonstrators. Newsmen imagined the shift in tactics would soon extend well beyond New York, where it first took hold. One article correctly predicted that there would "be no suffrage granted to women until the women themselves in great number demand it."

## CHAPTER 4

# TURNING UP THE HEAT

In the early 20th century, American suffragist Alice Paul (left) spent several years in England, where she worked closely with British suffragists.

BRITISH SUFFRAGISTS GAVE THE American suffrage movement a burst of energy. But one result of the women making their point so publicly was that they often clashed with police. NAWSA leaders, however, had worked hard to build a respectable image. They wanted no part of the violence and arrests that seemed to follow the British suffragists. Instead, they often encouraged working women to press peacefully for changes to voting laws in as many states and cities as possible.

**Harriot Blatch was unafraid of voicing her opinions about women's equality in large public gatherings.**

## Allies from Abroad

Harriot Blatch and the Equality League, on the other hand, embraced the British methods of fighting for voting rights. Blatch invited British suffragist Anne Cobden-Sanderson to address the league in New York. Cobden-Sanderson had been imprisoned for demonstrating in England. Her presentation energized the women of the Equality League. She convinced them of the value of public rallies and parades. By the beginning of 1908, New York suffragists were holding large rallies outside City Hall at least once a week. Newspapers took note of their efforts. The suffrage movement had become big news, and many people bought papers to keep up with the latest developments.

These bold strategies also challenged traditional understandings of womanhood. These women actively sought public attention, resisted male authority, and spoke their minds. The militant approach also increased the commitment of suffragists to the movement. Showing disrespect for traditional ladylike behavior by dressing unconventionally or smoking in public gave suffragists a sense of shared identity. Those who were arrested for demonstrating became heroes to the movement.

# A VIEW FROM ABROAD

British suffragists went to extreme measures in the struggle for women's suffrage in their own country. They were known for smashing shop windows and burning the homes of political opponents. They even bombed Westminster Abbey, a famous British landmark. British suffragists burned churches when ministers spoke out against them and spit on policemen who tried to arrest them. One suffragist, Mary Leigh, was even arrested for throwing a hatchet at a government official in 1912. British suffragists thought their American allies needed to adopt these more violent tactics to achieve their objective.

## Marching Toward Suffrage

Between 1910 and 1913, suffragists organized annual parades to draw attention to their cause. The first parade in New York City was small, but in 1912, 20,000 women marched in the parade. More than half a million spectators lined the parade route. That same year, NAWSA scored victories in Oregon, Arizona, and Kansas.

Also that year, presidential candidate Theodore Roosevelt supported women's suffrage in his campaign. Though Roosevelt lost the election, his support made women's suffrage a major political issue. Women were finally gaining the recognition they needed to move their idea for a constitutional amendment forward.

In 1913, suffragists turned up the heat by staging a parade in Washington, D.C., on the eve of President Woodrow Wilson's **inauguration**. The driving force behind the parade

**Theodore Roosevelt's Progressive Party was the first political party to campaign in support of women's suffrage.**

**The 1913 suffragist parade in Washington, D.C., drew a massive crowd of spectators, many of whom attacked the women as they marched.**

was Alice Paul, who had returned from helping British suffragists in 1912. The parade was led by suffragists from nations where women had already won the vote. A huge crowd of American working women followed them. Within a few blocks, crowds of angry men pressed in on the marchers. The men cursed at and insulted the suffragists. Women were pushed and tripped. Police did little to protect them. Meanwhile, Woodrow Wilson arrived at a nearly empty train station. Everyone was watching the spectacle of the parade.

# YESTERDAY'S HEADLINES

216       THE MARCH TO WASHINGTON

THE SPIRIT OF '13          THE SPIRIT OF 1913

The suffragists' 1913 march in Washington, D.C., made headlines across the nation. Newspaper cartoonists compared the marchers to the colonial army that had fought for America's independence in the Revolutionary War. They drew cartoons based on well-known paintings such as *Washington Crossing the Delaware* and *Spirit of '76*. However, their drawings substituted women for the Revolutionary War soldiers in the paintings. In this way, suffragists were linked in newspaper readers' minds to the principles of liberty and equality that the nation was founded upon.

Despite constant attacks and insults, the suffragists completed the parade route. The nation could not stop talking about them. The public was outraged by the attacks on the marchers. This created widespread sympathy for suffragists. The *New York Times* described the parade as "one of the most impressively beautiful spectacles ever staged in this country."

## World At War

Less than two weeks after the Washington march, Alice Paul and other suffragists visited President Wilson. They hoped to encourage him to support a women's voting amendment. Wilson responded that he did not consider women's suffrage to be a major issue. The suffragists left the meeting disappointed that Wilson had promised them nothing. However, they continued to pursue establishing women's right to vote in states that had no laws in place. By year's end, Illinois allowed women to vote in presidential, but not state, elections.

In 1914, Americans' attention was drawn away from the suffragists when World War I (1914–1918) erupted in Europe. Most suffragists did not support the United States' participation in the war. Many, including Jane Addams, spoke out against U.S. involvement.

**Millions of U.S. troops traveled abroad to fight during World War I.**

In January 1917, a large group of suffragists camped out at the White House gate in silent protest of the war. President Wilson ignored their demonstrations for six months. During that time, the protesters harshly criticized Wilson's policy on the war.

By June, policemen began arresting the suffragists and imprisoning them. Many of the imprisoned suffragists were mistreated. Guards beat, choked, and kicked the women. In protest of this treatment, the women began a hunger strike. When they grew weak and still refused to eat, guards force-fed them. When news of the suffragists' treatment leaked out, the women were released.

**Many suffragists were arrested as they protested outside of the White House in 1917.**

# A FIRSTHAND LOOK AT
## THE 19TH AMENDMENT

The 19th Amendment to the U.S. Constitution guaranteed that voting rights could no longer be denied based on gender. More than a century after the country's founding, women were finally granted constitutionally protected voting rights. See page 60 for a link to read the full amendment online.

## An Amendment on the Horizon

By January 1918, President Wilson had changed his position on the issue of women's suffrage. He announced his backing of an amendment to give women voting rights. Much of the nation was now solidly behind the women. Congress sensed the shift in public opinion. It passed the 19th Amendment in June 1919. The amendment then made its way to state legislatures, where it would have to be ratified by 36 states to become law.

By the summer of 1920, 35 states had ratified the amendment. The Tennessee legislature gathered in August 1920 to vote. With the vote tied at 48, the outcome rested on the shoulders of 24-year-old Harry Burn, the state's youngest representative. Burn had planned to vote against the amendment. Shortly before the voting began, however, he received a telegram from his mother. In the message, she asked him to "vote for suffrage" and "be a good boy." Out of respect for his mother's wish, Burn changed his vote. With that, the 19th Amendment was ratified. After decades of struggle, women had finally won the right to vote.

## MAP OF THE EVENTS

# What Happened Where?

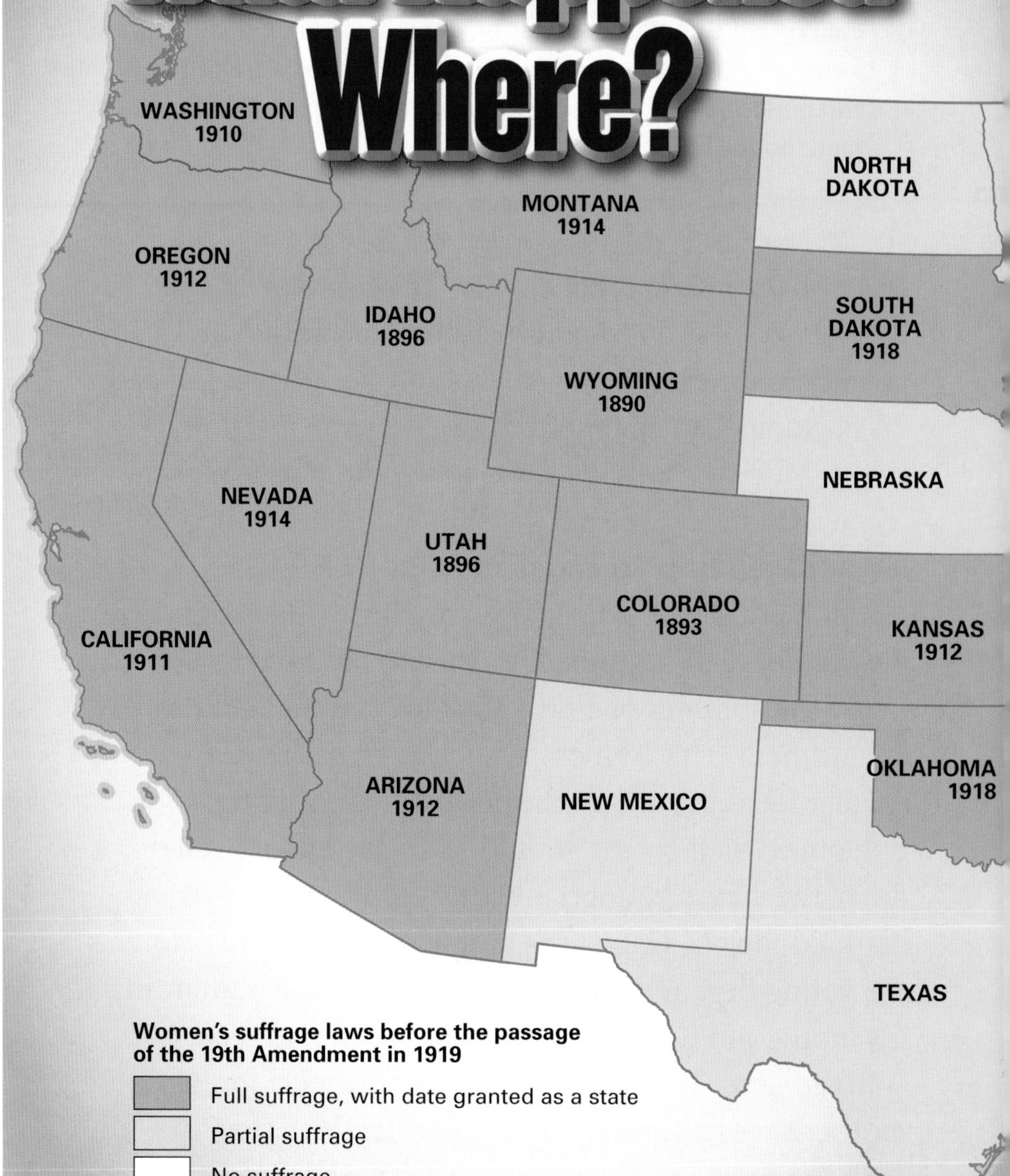
WASHINGTON 1910
OREGON 1912
IDAHO 1896
MONTANA 1914
NORTH DAKOTA
SOUTH DAKOTA 1918
WYOMING 1890
NEBRASKA
NEVADA 1914
UTAH 1896
COLORADO 1893
KANSAS 1912
CALIFORNIA 1911
ARIZONA 1912
NEW MEXICO
OKLAHOMA 1918
TEXAS
Women's suffrage laws before the passage of the 19th Amendment in 1919
Full suffrage, with date granted as a state
Partial suffrage
No suffrage

MINNESOTA

WISCONSIN

MICHIGAN
1918

IOWA

ILLINOIS

INDIANA

OHIO

MISSOURI

KENTUCKY

ARKANSAS

TENNESSEE

MISSISSIPPI

ALABAMA

GEORGIA

LOUISIANA

FLORIDA

VERMONT

MAINE

NH

NEW YORK
1917

MA

RI

CT

PENNSYLVANIA

NEW JERSEY

DELAWARE

MARYLAND

WEST
VIRGINIA

VIRGINIA

NORTH
CAROLINA

SOUTH
CAROLINA

N
W E
S

0    100    200 mi

0    100    200 km

# An Ongoing Battle

**After her Equal Rights Amendment was rejected by Congress in 1923, Alice Paul began working toward spreading the suffragist message around the world.**

Ratification of the 19th Amendment had major consequences for the United States. Political parties were forced to campaign on issues that were important to women. As a result, maternal rights, public education, and prohibition of alcohol became important political issues in the early 20th century.

Women's suffrage was only the beginning of the struggle for equality. In 1923, Alice Paul introduced an Equal Rights Amendment. The amendment would guarantee equal rights for men and women. It did not receive congressional approval until 1972, and it was never ratified. In many jobs, women still are not rewarded with equal pay for equal work. There are also fewer women than men in elected offices. Even though women's representation in Congress is steadily increasing, only 78 of 435 representatives are women. Of the nation's 100 senators, 20 are women. The dreams of suffragists such as Susan B. Anthony and Alice Paul await completion. However, their achievements have blazed the trail for women to continue working toward true equality in the United States.

**Though women are increasingly occupying more of the U.S. government's highest positions, no woman has ever been chosen as a major political party's presidential candidate. In the 2008 election, Hillary Clinton came closer than any previous female candidate.**

WAS ELECTED IN 1932.

# INFLUENTIAL INDIVIDUALS

Lucretia Mott

Frances Willard

**Lucretia Mott** (1793–1880) was an abolitionist and champion of women's rights who helped organize the Seneca Falls Convention.

**Sojourner Truth** (ca. 1797–1883) was a former slave who later spoke out in support of abolition. She was also a champion of women's rights.

**Elizabeth Cady Stanton** (1815–1902) was an abolitionist and suffragist who was the main author of the Declaration of Sentiments. She was one of the most important leaders of the American suffrage movement.

**Susan B. Anthony** (1820–1906) was a tireless and fearless campaigner for women's suffrage. In 1873, she was put on trial for voting illegally in the previous year's election.

**Frances Willard** (1839–1898) was the leader of the Woman's Christian Temperance Union. She linked the group with the fight for women's suffrage.

**Harriot Stanton Blatch** (1856–1940) was the daughter of Elizabeth Cady Stanton. She helped recruit working-class women into the suffrage movement.

**Carrie Chapman Catt** (1859–1947) was the president of the National American Woman Suffrage Association. She was also the founder of the League of Women Voters.

Carrie Chapman Catt

**Jane Addams** (1860–1935) was a visionary social reformer who helped pioneer the idea of settlement houses with Chicago's Hull House.

**Alice Paul** (1885–1977) was a radical suffragist who led protests at the White House and helped organize the 1913 suffrage parade in Washington, D.C. She was also the chief architect of the Equal Rights Amendment.

# TIMELINE

## 1790
The U.S. Constitution is fully adopted.

## 1850
The first national Women's Rights Convention is held.

## 1851
Sojourner Truth gives her "Ain't I a Woman?" speech.

## 1875
The Supreme Court's ruling in *Minor v. Happersett* narrows options available to suffragists.

## 1876
**July 4**
Susan B. Anthony reads the Declaration of Rights at the Philadelphia Centennial Exposition.

## 1908
Suffragists begin holding outdoor rallies.

## 1912
Theodore Roosevelt supports women's suffrage in his presidential campaign.

## 1913
**March 3**
A suffrage parade is held in Washington, D.C.

## 1866

Susan B. Anthony and Elizabeth Cady Stanton form the American Equal Rights Association (AERA).

## 1869

AERA splits over whether to support the 15th Amendment, and the AWSA and NWSA are formed.

## 1872

Susan B. Anthony is arrested for illegally trying to vote.

## 1878

A women's voting rights amendment is proposed in Congress.

## 1880

The WCTU lends support to the women's suffrage movement.

## 1890

NAWSA is formed from a merger of the NWSA and AWSA.

## 1917–1919

Suffragists protest in front of the White House.

## 1919

The 19th Amendment passes in both houses of Congress.

## 1920

Tennessee becomes the 36th state to ratify the 19th Amendment, completing the amendment's adoption into the Constitution.

# LIVING HISTORY

Primary sources provide firsthand evidence about a topic. Witnesses to a historical event create primary sources. They include autobiographies, newspaper reports of the time, oral histories, photographs, and memoirs. A secondary source analyzes primary sources, and is one step or more removed from the event. Secondary sources include textbooks, encyclopedias, and commentaries. To view the following primary and secondary sources, go to www.factsfornow .scholastic.com. Enter the keywords **Women's Right to Vote** and look for the Living History logo Σ¡.

Σ¡ **The Declaration of Sentiments** Created at the first Women's Rights Convention in Seneca Falls, New York, the Declaration of Sentiments outlined a list of ways in which the U.S. government treated women unfairly. It is one of the founding documents of the women's suffrage movement.

Σ¡ *Muller v. Oregon* *Muller v. Oregon* was a landmark Supreme Court case in which the court ruled that women could not be forced to work long hours, because they were physically weaker than men. While the case was a victory for women's labor rights, it also set a legal precedent for courts to discriminate based on gender.

Σ¡ **The 19th Amendment** The 19th Amendment to the U.S. Constitution guarantees that voting rights cannot be withheld based on gender. While some states had already allowed women to vote by the time the amendment was ratified, it provided constitutional protection for all women's voting rights in the United States.

Σ¡ **Susan B. Anthony's 1874 Petition to Congress** Susan B. Anthony was arrested and tried for voting illegally in the 1872 election. For her crime, she was fined $100. Anthony refused to pay the fine, and in 1874 she petitioned Congress to have the fine removed from her record.

# RESOURCES

## Books

Bingham, Jane. *Women at War: The Progressive Era, World War I and Women's Suffrage, 1900–1920*. New York: Chelsea House, 2011.

Colman, Penny. *Elizabeth Cady Stanton and Susan B. Anthony: A Friendship That Changed the World*. New York: Henry Holt and Company, 2011.

Kent, Deborah. *Elizabeth Cady Stanton*. Berkeley Heights, NJ: Enslow Publishers, 2010.

Visit this Scholastic Web site for more information on women's right to vote:
www.factsfornow.scholastic.com
Enter the keywords **Women's Right to Vote**

# GLOSSARY

**abolition** (a-buh-LIH-shuhn) the official end of something, such as slavery

**coverture** (KUH-vur-chur) the practice of granting a husband control over his wife's legal rights

**inauguration** (in-aw-gyuh-RAY-shuhn) a formal ceremony in which a government official is sworn into office

**legislature** (LEJ-iss-lay-chur) the part of government that is responsible for making and changing laws

**militant** (MIL-uh-tuhnt) very aggressive or willing to use force to support a cause

**petition** (puh-TISH-uhn) a letter signed by many people asking those in power to change their policy or actions

**picketed** (PIK-it-id) stood outside of a place in protest, usually while carrying signs and shouting slogans to get attention

**ratification** (rat-uh-fi-KAY-shuhn) official approval

**reform** (ri-FORM) a change that is made to correct or improve something

**settlement houses** (SET-uhl-muhnt HOW-zuz) organizations that provided services to recently arrived people from foreign countries

**suffragists** (SUHF-rij-ists) people who fought for suffrage, or the right to vote

**temperance** (TEM-pur-uhns) a reduction in the use of alcoholic beverages

**territory** (TER-i-tor-ee) an area connected with or owned by a country that is outside the country's main borders

Page numbers in *italics* indicate illustrations.

## ABOUT THE AUTHOR

**Peter Benoit** is the author of dozens of books for Children's Press. He has written about American history, ancient civilizations, ecosystems, and more. He is also a historical reenactor, occasional tutor, and poet. He is a graduate of Skidmore College, with a degree in mathematics. Peter lives in Greenwich, New York, a few miles from the childhood home of Susan B. Anthony.